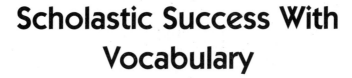

Scholastic Success With
Vocabulary

Grade 1

by Danette Randolph

New York • Toronto • London • Auckland • Sydney
Mexico City • New Delhi • Hong Kong • Buenos Aires

Teaching *Resources*

Cover art by Amy Vangsgard
Cover design by Maria Lilja
Interior illustrations by Carol Tiernon
Interior design by Quack & Company

ISBN 0-439-55379-2

Copyright © 2004 Scholastic, Inc.
All rights reserved. Printed in the U.S.A.

8 9 10   40   09 08

Introduction

Developing a rich vocabulary is an important key to learning. Students who have a wide vocabulary and become independent word learners score higher on achievement tests and are both successful in school and beyond. Parents and teachers alike will find this book a valuable teaching tool in helping students become independent word learners. Students will enjoy completing the activities as they encounter a vast and varied vocabulary including rhyming words, synonyms, antonyms, short vowel sounds, rhyming words, and much more. The activities are both engaging and educational. Take a look at the Table of Contents and you will feel rewarded knowing you're providing such a valuable resource for your students. Remember to praise them for their efforts and successes.

Table of Contents

Day by Day

Write the names of the missing days on each caterpillar. Then color each caterpillar using the color code.

Monday = red	Wednesday = green	Thursday = blue
Sunday = pink	Saturday = purple	Tuesday = orange
	Friday = yellow	

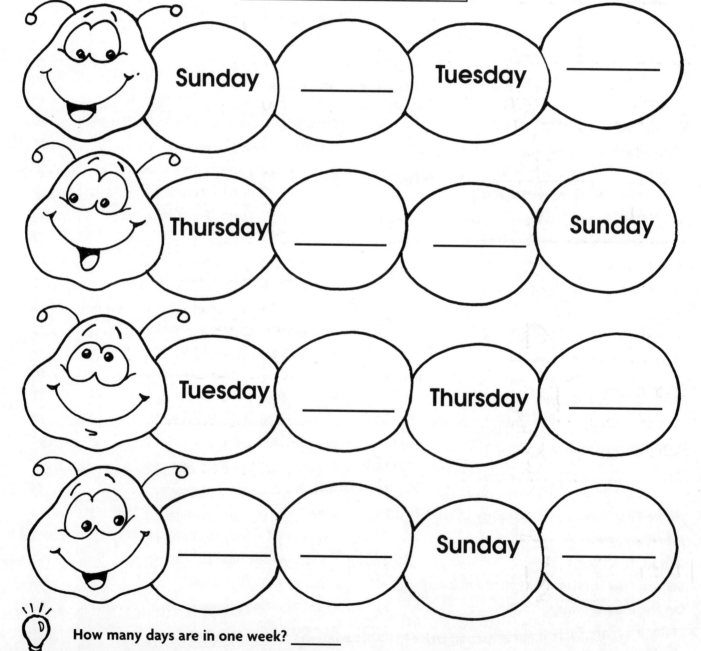

Sunday _____ Tuesday _____

Thursday _____ _____ Sunday

Tuesday _____ Thursday _____

_____ _____ Sunday _____

How many days are in one week? _____

Name _____

Month by Month

Read the chart. Write each answer.

January	Joe
February	Tina
March	Ben
April	Kara
May	James
June	Hallie
July	Shana
August	Juan
September	Kirk
October	Kate
November	Sarah
December	Dan

The first month of the year is _____.

The last month of the year is _____.

The month before March is _____.

The month between June and August is _____.

The month after May is _____.

When is my birthday?

Sarah   _____

Kirk   _____

Dan   _____

Kara   _____

Kate   _____

Hallie   _____

Ben   _____

Shana   _____

Scholastic Teaching Resources

 On another sheet of paper, write the abbreviation for each month.

Rhyme Time

Read the words in each row. Cross out the word that does not rhyme.
Write that word on the correct line below.

1. care   Cat   hair   there
2. were   cut   shut   nut
3. skate   alike   bait   late
4. bill   thrill   will   friends
5. not   bike   spike   like
6. play   say   day   were
7. sure   fur   but   her
8. and   ball   tall   call
9. end   bend   great   trend
10. hat   that   pat   they
11. hot   dot   Bear   cot
12. hand   still   sand   band

_____   _____   _____   _____
     1   8   11   2

_____   _____ ,   _____   _____
     5   3   7   10

_____   _____   _____   _____ !
     6   12   9   4

 On another sheet of paper, draw a picture of two words that rhyme with cat.

Name _____

Definitely Different

 Antonyms *are words with opposite meanings.*

Read the word on each flowerpot. Color the flower with the antonym.

 On another sheet of paper, draw a picture of the antonym for city.

Simply the Same

 Synonyms *are words with the same or nearly the same meanings.*

Read each word at the top of the box. Circle every other letter. Write the letters in order on the line to spell a synonym. The first one is done for you.

1. begin

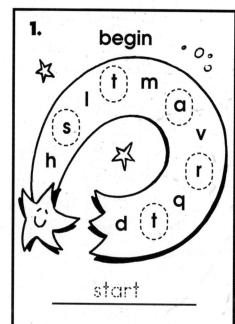

start
_____

2. glad

_____

3. loud

_____

4. little

_____

5. see

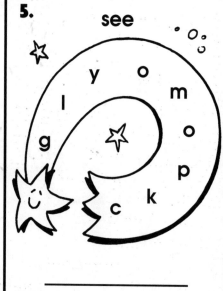

_____

6. big

_____

Name _____

Same but Different

 Homophones *are words that sound alike but are spelled differently and have different meanings.*

a	b	c	d	e	g	h	i	k	l	m	n	o	r	s	t	u	w	y
☺	🕐	➡	☆	★	⧖	❀	✋	✖	✓	◐	❀	⚑	⬜	⬧	❄	◆	✉	?

Use the code to write each homophone.

1. here ___ ___ ___ ___
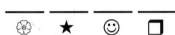

2. know ___ ___

3. to ___ ___ ___

4. ate ___ ___ ___ ___ ___

5. cent ___ ___ ___ ___ ___

6. break ___ ___ ___ ___ ___

7. so ___ ___ ___

8. main ___ ___ ___ ___

9. road ___ ___ ___ ___

Name _____

A Perfect Pair

 Compound words *are two words joined together to make a new word.*

Draw a line to connect the boxes to make compound words.
Write the compound word.

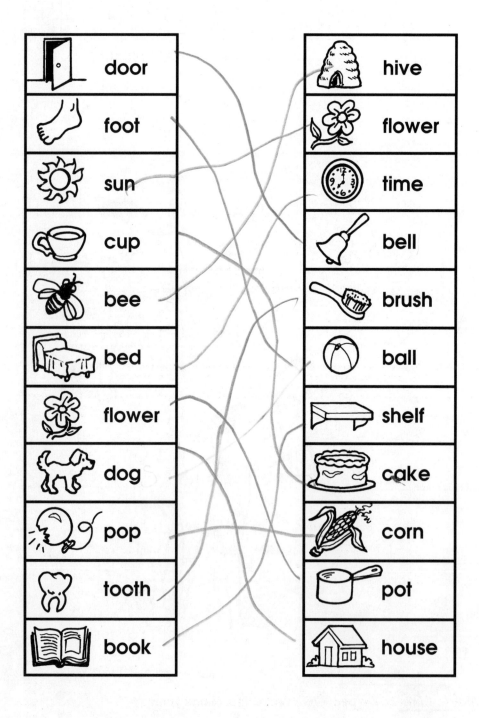

beehive
sun flower
bed time
door bell
tooth brush
football
book shelf
cup cake
pop corn

Dog House

Scholastic Teaching Resources

Perfect Shape

Unscramble the shape words. Write the words on the lines.

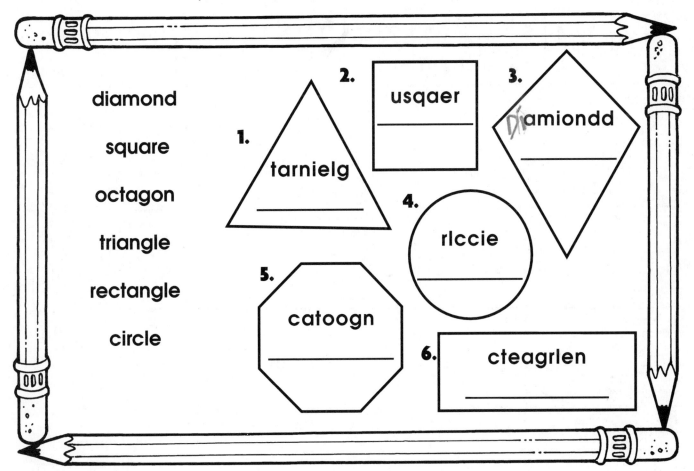

diamond

square

octagon

triangle

rectangle

circle

1. tarnielg _____

2. usqaer _____

3. Diamiondd _____

4. rlccie _____

5. catoogn _____

6. cteagrlen _____

What shape is a . . .

7. pizza? _Cirqe_

8. baseball infield? _Dimond_

9. tent? _triangle_

10.  stop sign? _OCtagon_

11. 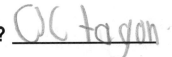 present? _Rectangle_

12. window? _Sqaure_

 Find eight things in your home that are shaped like a rectangle. Name them.

table, tv bed, Door, closit, poster box, and presents

Mystery Math Words

Use the code to identify the math words.

1	2	3	4	5	6	7	8	9	10	11	12	13	14	15	16	17	18	19	20
a	d	s	b	r	u	f	m	t	c	i	e	o	q	n	l	y	v	p	z

1.

$$\begin{array}{r} 2 \\ + 3 \\ \hline 5 \end{array}$$

$\overline{(1-0)}$ $\overline{(4-2)}$ $\overline{(1+1)}$

2.

$$\begin{array}{r} 3 \\ + 7 \\ \hline 10 \end{array}$$

$\overline{(1+2)}$ $\overline{(4+2)}$ $\overline{(12-4)}$

3.

$$\begin{array}{r} 5 \\ - 3 \\ \hline 2 \end{array}$$

$\overline{(9-6)}$ $\overline{(3+3)}$ $\overline{(7-3)}$ $\overline{(12-3)}$ $\overline{(10-5)}$ $\overline{(9-8)}$ $\overline{(3+7)}$ $\overline{(6+3)}$

4.

$$\begin{array}{r} 10 \\ - 7 \\ \hline 3 \end{array}$$

$\overline{(8-6)}$ $\overline{(15-4)}$ $\overline{(10-3)}$ $\overline{(3+4)}$ $\overline{(8+4)}$ $\overline{(2+3)}$ $\overline{(15-3)}$ $\overline{(10+5)}$ $\overline{(8+2)}$ $\overline{(11+1)}$

5.

$\overline{(8-5)}$ $\overline{(7+6)}$ $\overline{(8+8)}$ $\overline{(10+8)}$ $\overline{(7+5)}$

$2 + 3 = 5$

6.

$\overline{(10+2)}$ $\overline{(7+7)}$ $\overline{(10-4)}$ $\overline{(8-7)}$ $\overline{(9+7)}$

 On another sheet of paper, use the code to write math problems to spell the word *estimate.*

Scholastic Teaching Resources

Size It!

12 inches = 1 foot

3 feet = 1 yard

5,280 feet = 1 mile

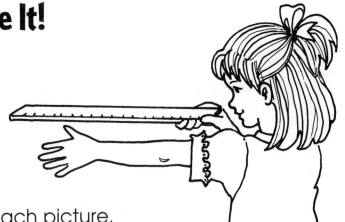

Write the best unit of measure for each picture.

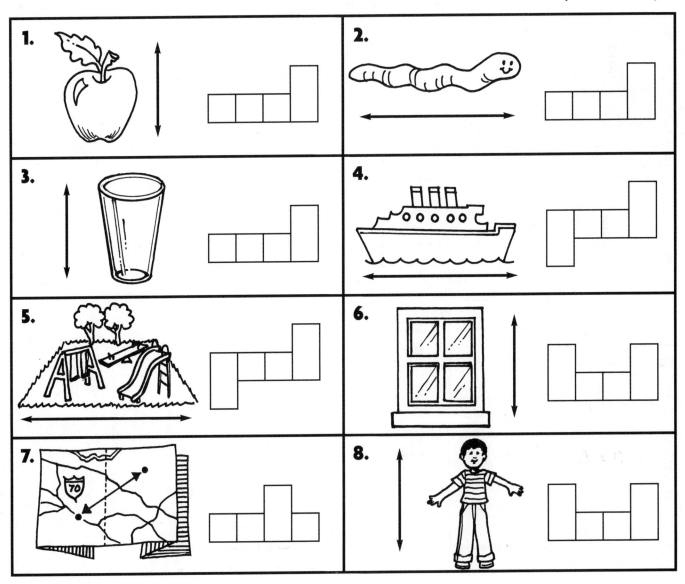

 Find out how many inches tall you are.

Metric Measurement Maze

10 centimeters (cm) = 1 decimeter (dm)

10 decimeters (dm) = 1 meter (m)

1,000 meters (m) = 1 kilometer (km)

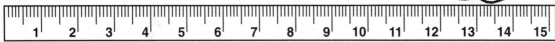

centimeters

Follow the maze to the best unit of measure for each picture.

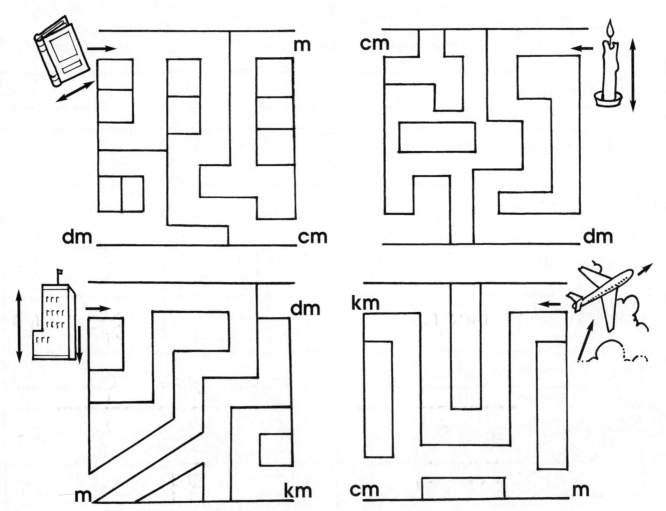

 Circle the unit of measurement that is largest.

meter   centimeter   kilometer   decimeter

The Four Seasons

Circle the season that goes with each sentence.

1. Birds make nests for babies.

2. Children build snowmen.

3. Leaves turn, red, orange, and yellow.

4. Children go swimming outside.

5. Flowers begin to bloom.

6. Some animals hibernate.

7. Trees start losing leaves.

8. Insects fly through the air.

 Did you notice a pattern in the answers? Draw the pattern in the squares.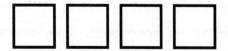

Scholastic Teaching Resources

Name _____

Weather Watchers

Look at the weather picture. Read the weather clue.
Cross out every other letter box. The letters left will
name the kind of weather. Write the weather word on the line.
The first one has been done or you.

I see nothing
but snow.

| b | e | l | n | i | s | z | a | z | i | a | o | r | f | d |

1. _____ blizzard _____

I see balls of ice
falling from the sky

| h | j | a | j | i | q | l |

2. _____

I see a dark funnel
cloud in the sky.

| t | r | o | p | r | b | n | g | a | j | d | u | o |

3. _____

I see water drops
falling from the sky.

| r | g | a | k | i | a | n |

4. _____

I see white flakes
falling from the sky.

| s | e | n | b | o | i | w |

5. _____

I see beautiful
blue skies.

| s | f | u | s | n | c | s | l | h | o | i | r | n | r | e |

6. _____

Beautiful Babies

Cross out every other letter to name the baby animal. Write the name on the line. The first one has been done for you.

k	~~j~~	i	~~u~~	t	~~g~~	t	~~b~~	e	~~s~~	n

1. _kitten_

l	v	a	g	m	c	b

2. _____

t	h	a	t	d	a	p	k	o	r	l	f	e

3. _____

d	f	u	j	c	w	k	d	l	n	i	k	n	o	g

4. _____

f	c	a	i	w	d	n

5. _____

c	e	u	x	b

6. _____

c	l	a	d	l	n	f

7. _____

p	d	i	h	g	y	l	i	e	b	t

8. _____

c	o	h	r	i	e	c	q	k

9. _____

p	b	u	u	p	a	p	z	y

10. _____

 Find out the name of a baby penguin. _____

Scholastic Teaching Resources

All Kinds of Animals

Read each clue. Write the names of the correct animals in the crossword puzzle.

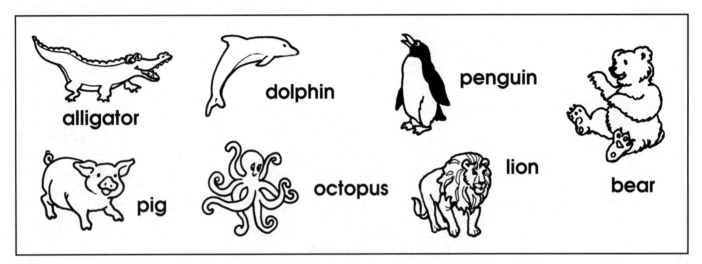

alligator
dolphin
penguin
bear
pig
octopus
lion

Across

2. This mammal hibernates in the winter.

5. This reptile has a long nose and sharp teeth.

6. This mammal makes an oink sound.

7. This mammal has a mane.

Down

1. This bird uses its wings to swim.

3. This mammal lives like a fish.

4. This sea creature has eight arms.

 On another sheet of paper, draw a picture of your favorite animal. Write one sentence about it.

Scholastic Teaching Resources

Inspect the Insects

Use the words in the box to identify the parts of an insect.

leg	antenna	wing	head	abdomen	thorax

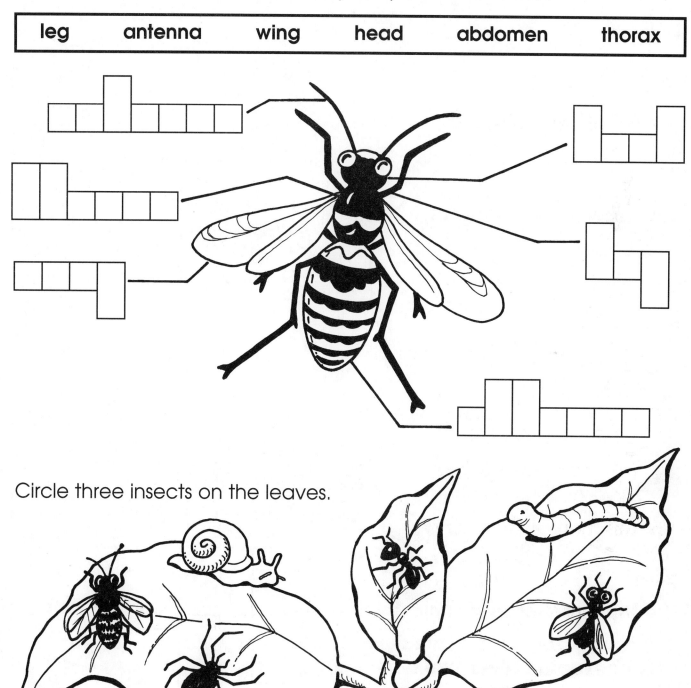

Circle three insects on the leaves.

 Did you know that insects have only six legs? That is why a spider is not an insect. Use a reference book to find out another fact about insects.

Name That Dinosaur

Write the dinosaur name that goes with each clue.

I am one of the longest dinosaurs.

— — — — — — —
     6   4

I am the fiercest dinosaur.

— — — — — — — — — — — —
3   2

I am a spike-tailed dinosaur.

— — — — — — — — —
  7

I am a three-horned dinosaur.

— — — — — — — — —
        1

I am a duck-billed dinosaur.

— — — — — — — — —
        5

Use the letters above to finish the rhyme.

**Dinosaurs were amazing creatures, I think
But I'll never see a real one because they are . . .**

◯ ◯ ◯ ◯ ◯ ◯ ◯ !
1 2 3 4 5 6 7

Trachodon

Brachiosaurus

**Tyrannosaurus
rex**

Triceratops

Stegosaurus

Scholastic Teaching Resources

Name _____

Fanciful Flowers

Use the words to label the picture. Then use the shape code to complete the sentence below.

s⧄eed   stem   fl⬚wer   rai⬡n   le⬳f
roo⬡t s   so⬚l   ⬡bug   sunligh⬡t

A person who enjoys learning about flowers is a

        .

Out of This World

Use the grid to identify each planet.

	A	B	C
3	Neptune	Earth	Mars
2	Uranus	Saturn	Venus
1	Mercury	Jupiter	Pluto

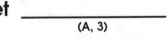

The third planet from the sun is _____.
(B, 3)

Seven rings circle _____.
(B, 2)

_____ is called the "Red Planet."
(C, 3)

_____ is the planet closest to the sun.
(A, 1)

The smallest planet is _____.
(C, 1)

The only planet tipped on its side is _____.
(A, 2)

A planet often called a morning or an evening star is _____.
(C, 2)

_____ is a giant ball of gas.
(B, 1)

A day lasts only 16 hours on the planet _____.
(A, 3)

 Choose the planet you would most like to visit. On another sheet of paper, write two reasons why you would like to go there.

Scholastic Teaching Resources

Sensational Service

Read each clue. Write the name of each community helper.

1. I give you a checkup each year as you grow up.
 	
_ _ _ _ _ _
     5
	2. I drive a vehicle that is really cool. I pick you up each day for school.
	
	_ _ _ _ _ _ _ _ _ _
	     6

3. When smoke hits your nose I'll come with my hose.
 	
_ _ _ _ _ _ _ _ _ _ _
     2
	4. I work on your teeth awhile, so you can have a bright smile.
	
	_ _ _ _ _ _ _
	     4

5. I share a lot for you to learn, and in my class we all take turns.
 	
_ _ _ _ _ _ _
   1
	6. I am here to help you look for an interesting book.
	
	_ _ _ _ _ _ _ _
	     3

Use the letters from above to finish the sentence.

For all you do, we say . . .

__ __ __ __ k y __ __!
1 2 3 4   5 6

bus driver	doctor	dentist
librarian	firefighter	teacher

On the Move

Circle the transportation words. The words go across and down.

airplane

sailboat

van

bus

ship

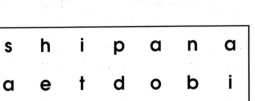

s	h	i	p	a	n	a
a	e	t	d	o	b	i
i	l	s	v	a	i	r
l	i	t	a	k	k	p
b	c	a	n	o	e	l
o	o	e	r	c	f	a
a	p	u	c	a	r	n
t	t	r	u	c	k	e
r	e	v	h	b	u	s
t	r	a	i	n	l	s

car

canoe

train

helicopter

truck

bike

Complete the chart to identify different kinds of transportation.

air	land	water
_____	_____	_____
_____	_____	_____
	_____	
	_____	
	_____	

Making a Map

Use the code to fill in the blanks about parts of a map.

a	b	c	e	h	k	l	m	n	o	p	r	s	t	u	w	y
↖	✹	○	❄	●	✪	✦	☑	➸	❀	⚙	☊	◄	⊙	◷	☺	↗

1. A map ___ ___ ___ ___ ___ ___ is a

◄ ↗ ☑ ✹ ❀ ✦
picture that stands for a real thing.

2. A list of symbols and what they stand

for is called the ___ ___ ___ ___ ___ ___.

☑ ↖ ⚙ ✪ ❄ ↗

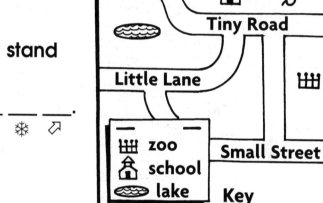

3. The cardinal directions are

___ ___ ___ ___ ___, ___ ___ ___ ___ ___,

➸ ❀ ☊ ⊙ ●   ◄ ❀ ◷ ⊙ ●

___ ___ ___ ___, and ___ ___ ___ ___.

❄ ↖ ◄ ⊙   ☺ ❄ ◄ ⊙

4. The ___ ___ ___ ___ ___ ___ ___ ___ ___ ___ ___ ___

○ ❀ ☑ ❄ ↖ ◄ ◄   ☊ ❀ ◄ ❄
shows the cardinal directions on a map.

 A book of maps is called an atlas. Spell *atlas* **using the code above.**

Getting Around Town

Use the map to complete the crossword puzzle.

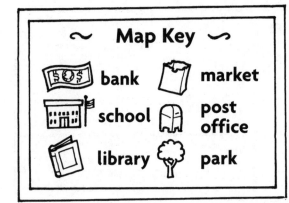

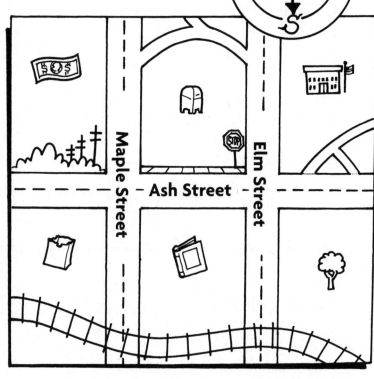

Across

3. the first street crossed if walking west from the park

5. the direction to travel from the market to the bank

6. the direction to travel from the post office to the school

north   south   east   west

Down

1. the direction to travel from the library to the market

2. the first street crossed if walking east from the bank

4. the direction to travel from the school to the park

7. the street crossed if walking north from the library

 On another sheet of paper, make a map of an imaginary city just for kids.

Scholastic Teaching Resources

Name _____

Easy Economics

Unscramble the money words. Write the words.

neynp	lradlo	mdie
1. _____	2. _____	3. _____
nlkice	**Word Bank** quarter penny nickel dime dollar	urtaqre
4. _____		5. _____

A **need** is something you must have to live. A **want** is something you do not need to live. Color the circles with wants.

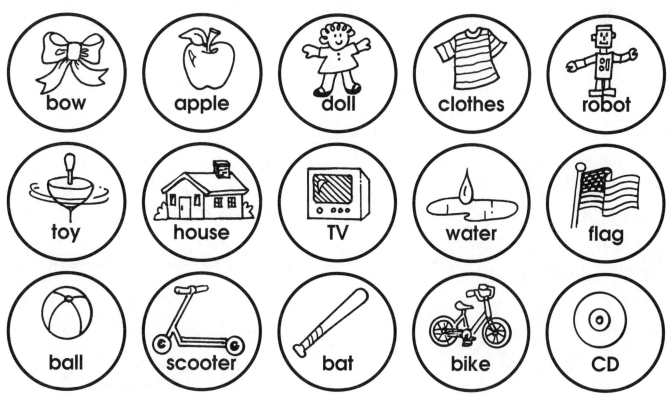

bow   apple   doll   clothes   robot

toy   house   TV   water   flag

ball   scooter   bat   bike   CD

On another sheet of paper, draw a picture of something you really want but do not need.

Ever-Changing Emotions

Begin at the star. Move around the circle and color the spaces with odd numbers. Then go back to the star. Write the letters above the spaces you did not color in order on the line below each face.

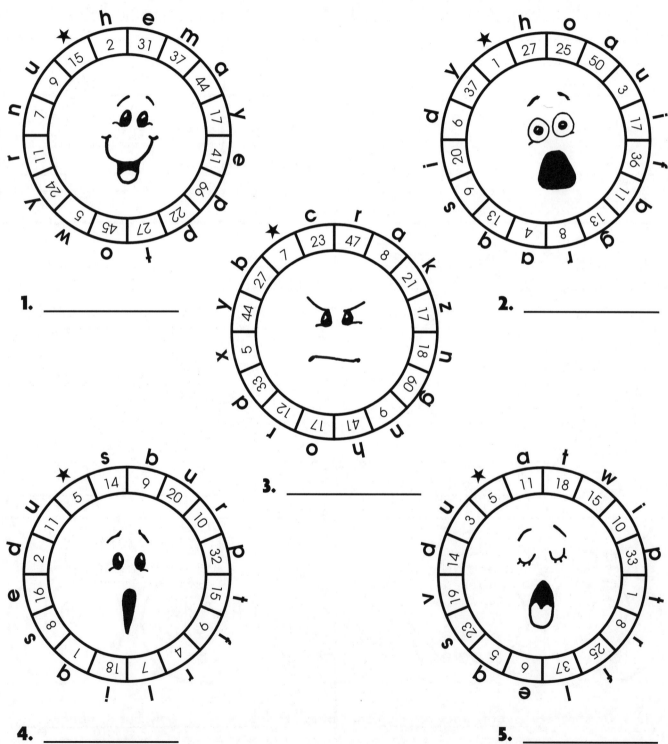

1. _____

2. _____

3. _____

4. _____

5. _____

Name _____

Name _____

Character Counts!

Use a word from the box to describe the character trait shown in each picture.

| polite | cooperative | helpful | honest | responsible | kind |

I finished my homework all by myself.

1. _____

Sir, I think you dropped a five dollar bill.

2. _____

Dad, I'll take out the trash.

3. _____

We make a good team!

4. _____

Would you like one of my cookies?

COOKIES

5. _____

Thank you for the ice cream, Mom.

6. _____

Scholastic Teaching Resources

Awesome A Words

Complete the crossword puzzle using the words from the Word Bank.
The words all have the short-*a* sound.

Across

2. a grown kitten
3. used in baseball
4. another name for sack
6. a baby cow
8. something to eat

Down

1. something worn on your head
2. a taxi
3. opposite of white
5. opposite of sad
7. a boy
8. opposite of happy

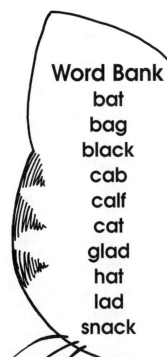

Word Bank
bat
bag
black
cab
calf
cat
glad
hat
lad
snack

On another sheet of paper, draw a silly picture using
words with the short-*a* sound.

Scholastic Teaching Resources

Name _____

Excellent E Words

Unscramble the short-e words. Use the words to complete each sentence below.

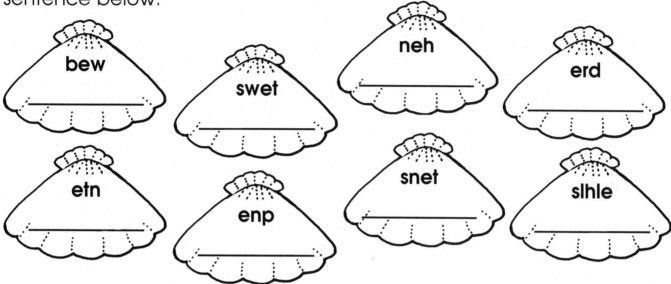

bew

swet

neh

erd

etn

enp

snet

slhle

1. I rhyme with swell. I am a pretty _____.

2. I rhyme with bed. I am the color _____.

3. I rhyme with Deb. I am a spider's _____.

4. I rhyme with test. I am the direction _____.

5. I rhyme with den. I am a ballpoint _____.

6. I rhyme with let. I am a butterfly _____.

7. I rhyme with best. I am a bird's _____.

8. I rhyme with ten. I am a chicken or _____.

 On another sheet of paper, draw a picture of something else whose name has the short-e sound.

Fishy I Words

Read each clue in the fishbowl. Find the fish with the correct answer. Color both fish the same color to show a match.

1. a big boat
2. to hope for something
3. part of a fish
4. to take a small drink
5. to tell a lie
6. a part of your mouth
7. the top of a pan
8. a small haircut

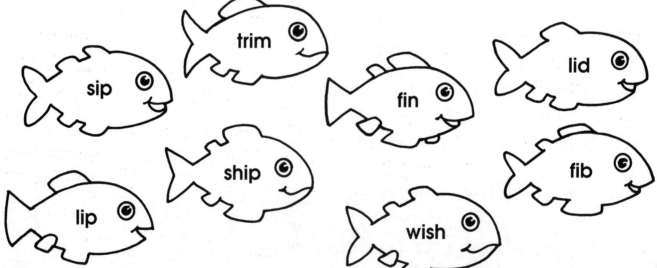

💡 **The whale shark is the largest fish in the ocean. On another sheet of paper, draw a picture of what you think it looks like.**

Scholastic Teaching Resources

Name _____

Outrageous O Words

Read each word. If it has the short-*o* sound, color the ball blue. If it does not have the short-*o* sound, color the ball green.

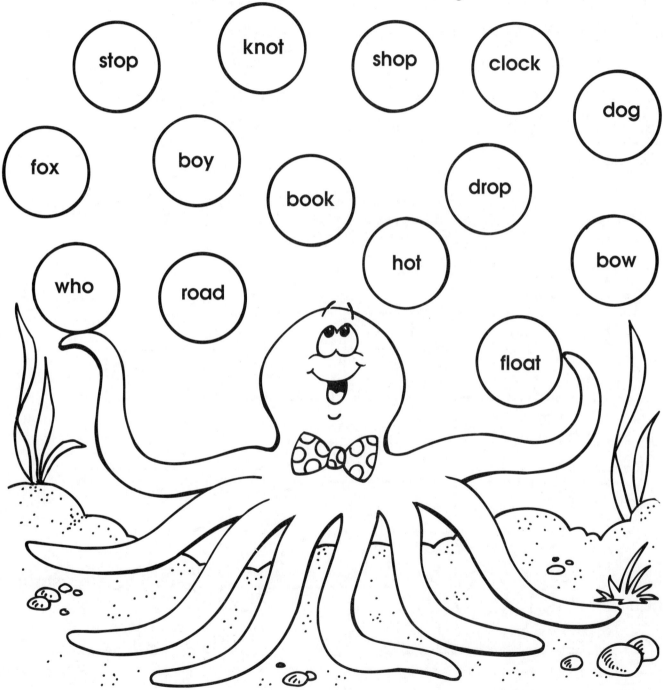

stop

knot

shop

clock

dog

fox

boy

book

drop

who

road

hot

bow

float

 Most sea animals have fins and flippers to help them swim. Find out how an octopus moves through the water.

Fun With Short-U Words

Use the clues to connect the dots in the order of the clues.

1. a small insect
2. something squirrels eat
3. part of a hamburger
4. a baby bear
5. opposite of down
6. to cry and complain
7. scissors do this
8. ball of fire in the sky
9. something to wipe feet on
10. a bush
11. a big yellow _____

 On another sheet of paper, write a poem about a ride on a bus.

Hopping Fun

Use the picture clues to complete each puzzle with words that have short vowel sounds. Then use the number code to answer the riddle below.

net   mop   sun   fish   hand   pig   rug   ant   pencil   frog

What do you give a sick frog? A __ __ __ __ __ __ __ __ __ __ !

1 2 3 4 5 6 7 8 2 9

The Long and Short of It

Read each word. If the word has a long vowel sound, color the box red. If the word has a short vowel sound, color the box yellow. The colors will help you answer the riddle.

Hello!

Hi!

net	ant	hand	sun	rug	fish	run	pig
bus	play	me	mop	cub	five	see	stop
fox	cut	men	best	cat	hop	sip	pen
hat	wish	lid	smoke	tail	tent	red	bun
cut	then	hop	hot	up	hip	web	bag
nest	hope	nut	hen	bat	calf	snake	fin
black	top	cake	high	rain	mile	west	shop
trim	bed	nap	ship	fib	ten	tag	man

How can you say hello without words?

You can remember to ____ ____ ____ ____ ____ .

Scholastic Teaching Resources

Name _____

Nouns

Hop on Over

*A **noun** is a naming word. It names a person, place, or thing.*

Follow each frog's path across the pond to its lily pad.

Color the rocks that name people red.

Color the rocks that name places yellow.

Color the rocks that name things blue.

boy

school

banana

teacher

restaurant

envelope

doctor

library

car

desk

lady

store

box

nurse

gas station

post office

toy

clerk

hospital

shirt

vet

theater

book

Anchors Away!

 A **proper noun** *names a special person, place, or thing. It begins with a capital letter.*

Color the proper nouns to connect the boat and anchor.

Dean	lady	country	astronaut
school	New York	dog	team	car
boy	Jenna	sport	girl	house
street	North Street	store	song	bird
friend	Mars	John Glenn	America	Elm Grove School
motorcycle	cat	paint	man	April
planet	soda	ocean	bed	

Scholastic Teaching Resources

Time for Action

→ *A* **verb** *is a word that shows action.*

Read each word. Color the leaves with action words to help the monkey get to the bananas.

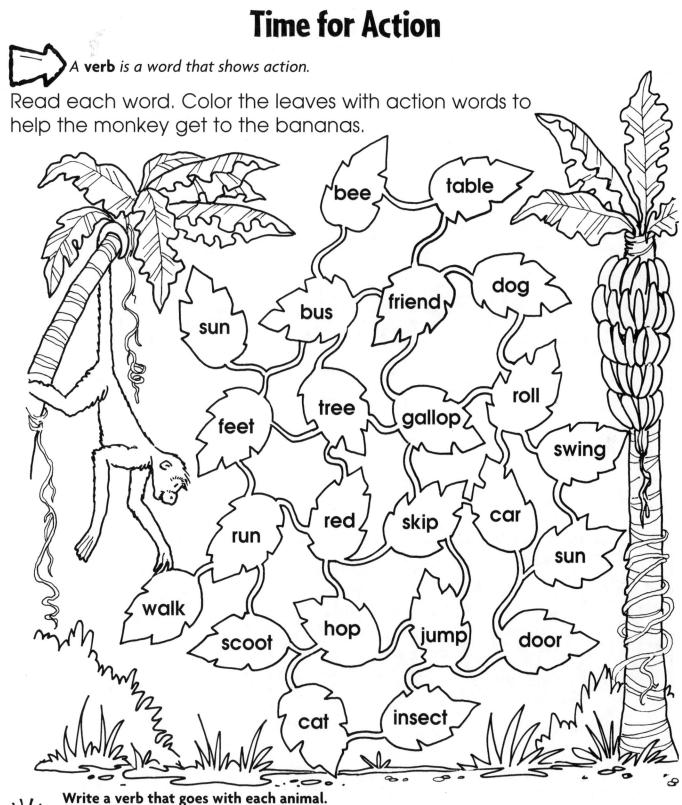

bee · table · sun · bus · friend · dog · feet · tree · gallop · roll · swing · run · red · skip · car · sun · walk · scoot · hop · jump · door · cat · insect

Write a verb that goes with each animal.

rabbit _____   eagle _____   cat _____

skunk _____   snake _____   bear _____

Describe That

 *An **adjective** is a describing word.*

Begin at the star. Follow the directions. Then write the circled letters in order on the blanks to spell a describing word.

Circle every third letter.

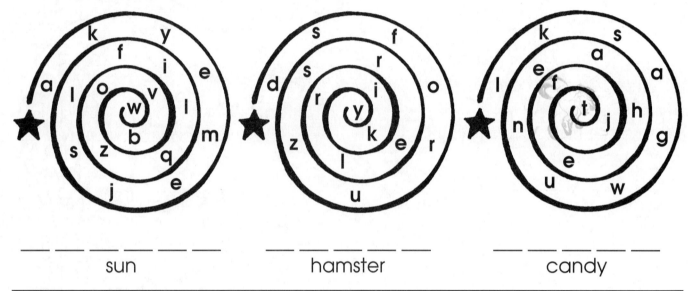

___ ___ ___   ___ ___ ___ ___ ___ ___   ___ ___ ___ ___ ___

  sun   hamster   candy

Circle every fourth letter.

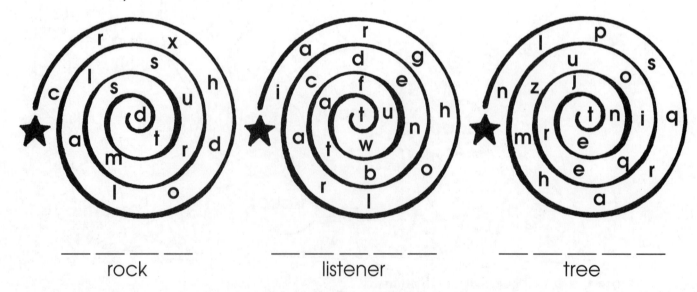

___ ___ ___ ___   ___ ___ ___ ___   ___ ___ ___ ___

  rock   listener   tree

On another sheet of paper, write an adjective to describe each member of your family.

How Do You Do It?

 *An **adverb** is a word that tells how, when, or where an action takes place.*

Begin at the star. Color the spaces with odd numbers. Then go back to the star. Write the letters you did not color in order on the line to finish each sentence.

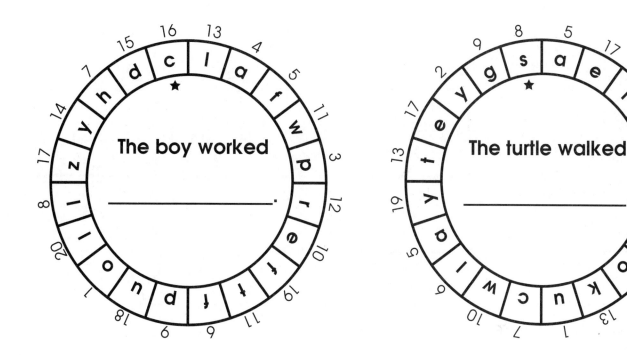

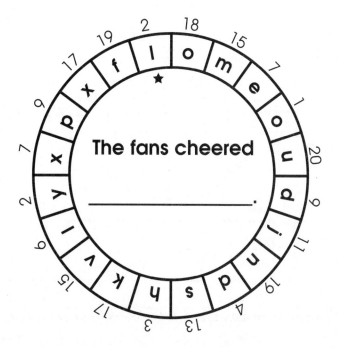

A Perfect Fit

 A **contraction** is a word made from two words. One or more letters are left out. An **apostrophe** (') is used in the place of the missing letter or letters.

 have   am  are  would   is   not   will

Write the word used to make each contraction.

1. she'll
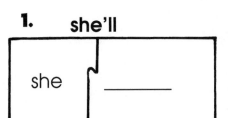
she ____

2. I've
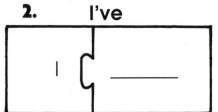
I ____

3. we're
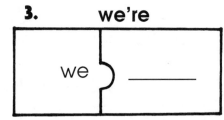
we ____

4. they're
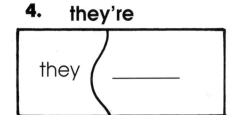
they ____

5. could've
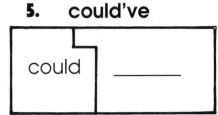
could ____

6. they'll
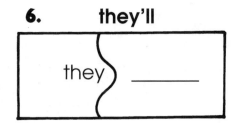
they ____

7. we'd
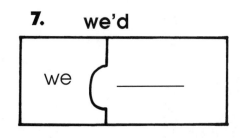
we ____

8. I'm
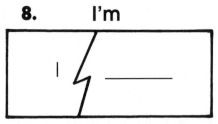
I ____

9. he'd
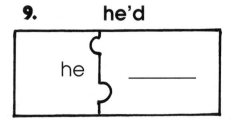
he ____

10. aren't
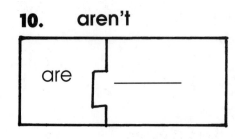
are ____

11. it's
it ____

12. won't
will ____

Say It in a Letter

Use the code to write the names of each part of the letter.

a	b	c	d	e	g	i	l	n	o	r	s	t	u	y
⊙	↗	⌘	☺	✶	⊠	💧	🕐	■	❖	❄	📫	○	✦	🌀

1. ⊠❄✶✶○💧■⊠   **2.** ☺⊙○✶

_____   _____

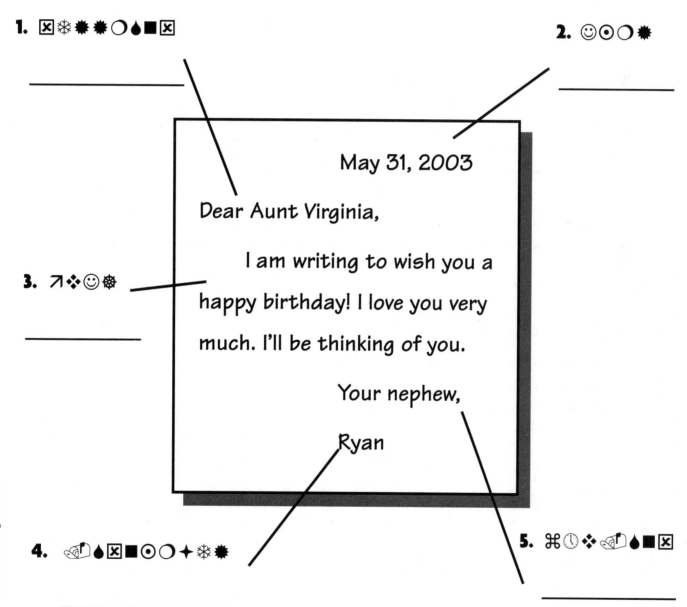

May 31, 2003

Dear Aunt Virginia,

    I am writing to wish you a happy birthday! I love you very much. I'll be thinking of you.

        Your nephew,

Ryan

3. ↗❖☺🌀

_____

4. 📫💧⊠■⊙○✦❄✶   **5.** ⌘🕐❖📫💧■⊠

_____   _____

 Have someone help you write a thank-you letter on another sheet of paper.

Stretching for Snacks

Finish each analogy using the Word Bank. Write the word on the line.

1. *Shut* is to *open* as *soft* is to _____.

2. *Knee* is to *leg* as *elbow* is to _____.

3.  *Airplane* is to *pilot* as *bus* is to _____.

4.  *Lime* is to *green* as *lemon* is to _____.

5. *Sink* is to *wash* as *oven* is to _____.

Word Bank

bake	yellow
hard	arm	driver

Scholastic Teaching Resources

Analogy Maze

Complete each analogy using a word from the box. Color each word to show the path through the maze.

1. *Knife* is to *cut* as *pencil* is to _____.

2. *Pig* is to *squeal* as *dog* is to _____.

3. *Finger* is to *hand* as *toe* is to _____.

4. *Tall* is to *short* as *high* is to _____.

5. *Animal* is to *zoo* as *clown* is to _____.

6. *Wing* is to *bird* as *fin* is to _____.

7. *Juice* is to *drink* as *steak* is to _____.

8. *Cat* is to *meow* as *lion* is to _____.

9. *Smile* is to *frown* as *up* is to _____.

Roar!

Meow!

foot	fish	boy	fly	cook
hand	write	under	pet	sleep
elbow	bark	laugh	read	cut
flower	low	play	arm	knee
movie	roar	circus	eat	down

Word Relations

Write the missing word to complete each analogy. Color the words
below to help the elephant get to the camel.

1. *Knife* is to *cut* as *broom* is to _____.

2. *Early* is to *late* as *light* is to _____.

3. *Short* is to *tall* as *small* is to _____.

4. *Question* is to *answer* as *empty* is to _____.

5. *Quiet* is to *noisy* as *hot* is to _____.

6. *Shout* is to *whisper* as *wide* is to _____.

7. *Empty* is to *full* as *clean* is to _____.

8. *Boat* is to *water* as *plane* is to _____.

9. *In* is to *out* as *happy* is to _____.

10. *Elephant* is to *trunk* as *camel* is to _____.

Answer Key

Page 4
Monday, Wednesday;
Friday, Saturday;
Wednesday, Friday; Friday,
Saturday, Monday

Page 5
January; December;
February; July; June;
November, September,
December, April, October,
June, March, July

Page 6
1. Cat; 2. were; 3. alike;
4. friends; 5. not; 6. were;
7. but; 8. and; 9. great;
10. they; 11. Bear; 12. still;
Cat and Bear were not
alike, but they were still
great friends!

Page 7
up, big, in; boy, hot, over;
soft, ugly, sad

Page 8
2. happy; 3. noisy; 4. small;
5. look; 6. large

Page 9
1. hear; 2. no; 3. two;
4. eight; 5. scent; 6. brake;
7. sew; 8. mane; 9. rode

Page 10
doorbell, football,
sunflower, cupcake,
beehive, bedtime,
flowerpot, doghouse,
popcorn, toothbrush,
bookshelf

Page 11
1. triangle; 2. square;
3. diamond; 4. circle;
5. octagon; 6. rectangle;
7. circle, 8. diamond;
9. triangle, 10. octagon;
11. rectangle, 12. square

Page 12
1. add; 2. sum; 3. subtract;
4. difference; 5. solve;
6. equal

Page 13
1. inch; 2. inch; 3. inch;

4. yard; 5. yard; 6. foot;
7. mile; 8. foot

Page 14
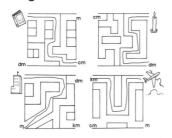

Page 15
1. spring; 2. winter; 2. fall;
3. summer; 4. spring;
5. winter; 6. fall; 7. summer

Page 16
2. hail; 3. tornado; 4. rain;
5. snow; 6. sunshine

Page 17
2. lamb; 3. tadpole;
4. duckling; 5. fawn; 6. cub;
7. calf; 8. piglet; 9. chick;
10. puppy

Page 18
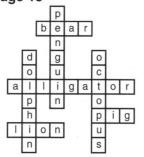

Page 19
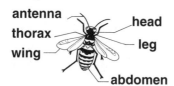

Page 20
Brachiosaurus,
Tyrannosaurus rex,
Stegosaurus, Triceratops,
Trachodon; extinct

Page 21
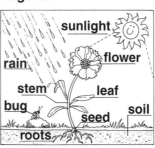

botanist

Page 22
Earth, Saturn, Mars,
Mercury, Pluto, Uranus,
Venus, Jupiter, Neptune

Page 23
1. doctor; 2. bus driver;
3. firefighter; 4. dentist;
5. teacher; 6. librarian;
thank you

Page 24
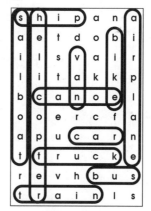

air: airplane, helicopter;
land: train, van, truck, bus,
car, bike; water: canoe,
ship, sailboat

Page 25
1. symbol; 2. map key;
3. north, south, east, west;
4. compass rose

Page 26
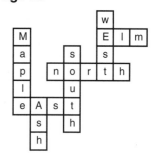

Page 27
1. penny; 2. dollar; 3. dime;
4. nickel; 5. quarter; The
following circles should be
colored: bow, doll, robot,
toy, TV, flag, ball, scooter,
bat, bike, CD

Page 28
1. happy; 2. afraid;
3. angry; 4. surprised;
5. tired

Page 29
Answers may vary.
Possible answers are:
1. responsible; 2. honest;
3. helpful; 4. cooperative;
5. kind; 6. polite

Page 30
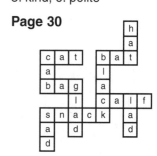

Page 31
1. shell; 2. red; 3. web;
4. west; 5. pen; 6. net;
7. nest; 8. hen

Page 32
1. ship; 2. wish; 3. fin;
4. sip; 5. fib; 6. lip;
7. lid; 8. trim

Scholastic Teaching Resources

Page 33

Page 34

1. bug; 2. nut; 3. bun;
4. cub; 5. up; 6. fuss;
7. cut; 8. sun; 9. rug;
10. shrub; 11. bus

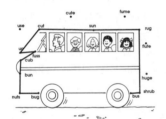

Page 35

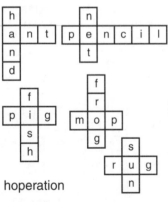

hoperation

Page 36

smile

Page 37

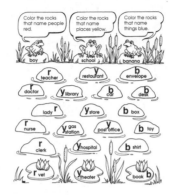

Page 38

Page 39

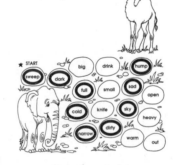

Page 40

yellow, furry, sweet; hard,
great, short

Page 41

carefully, slowly, loudly

Page 42

1. will; 2. have; 3. are;
4. are; 5. have; 6. will;
7. would; 8. am; 9. would;
10. not; 11. is; 12. not

Page 43

1. greeting; 2. date;
3. body; 4. signature;
5. closing

Page 44

1. hard; 2. arm; 3. driver;
4. yellow; 5. bake

Page 45

1. write; 2. bark; 3. foot;
4. low; 5. circus; 6. fish;
7. eat; 8. roar; 9. down

foot	fish	boy	fly	cook
hand	write	under	pet	sleep
elbow	bark	laugh	read	cut
flower	low	play	arm	knee
movie	roar	circus	eat	down

Page 46

1. sweep; 2. dark; 3. big;
4. full; 5. cold; 6. narrow;
7. dirty; 8. sky 9. sad;
10. hump